SI ONLINE

Multimedia Resources for
**TEACHERS
STUDENTS
PARENTS**

SOUND INNOVATIONS

CREATIVE WARM-UPS

Exercises for Intonation, Rhythm, Bowing, and Creativity

INTERMEDIATE STRING ORCHESTRA

Bob **PHILLIPS** | Kirk **MOSS** | Matt **TURNER** | Stephen **BENHAM**

The levels of this book focus on four important aspects of string performance and can be used in any order as either warm-ups or structured units. This material is an ideal complement to *SI Sound Development for Intermediate String Orchestra*. Video and audio demonstrations of key skills, along with additional supplemental material, can be accessed at **alfred.com/CreativeWarmUps**.

Level 1: Sound Intonation

These innovative intonation exercises in the most common keys will develop high-level listening skills through practicing intervals, chord tones and balance, major/minor/diminished/augmented chord qualities, drones, extended hand patterns—including cello extension pedagogy—and Bach chorales.

Level 2: Sound Rhythms

The structured rhythmic patterns in Level 2 provide opportunities to analyze, audiate, compose, notate, and perform rhythms that emphasize rhythmic independence and develop rhythmic ensemble playing in large-group settings.

Level 3: Sound Bowing Fluency and Choreography

Bowing fluency and choreography will refine technique, leading to a characteristic, beautiful sound. These warm-ups focus on playing in all parts of the bow, starting in different points of the bow, using expressive bow strokes, and executing fluid string crossings.

Level 4: Sound Creativity

This groundbreaking sequence of exercises and repertoire, ranging from a 17th-century *chaconne* to an Arabic/Turkish *taqsim*, helps develop improvisation and composition skills. The rhythm and melodic riff examples provide a toolbox of material to use while improvising in distinct styles—like classical, jazz, Latin, and rock— or over a drone accompaniment.

SI ONLINE

Multimedia Resources for
**TEACHERS
STUDENTS
PARENTS**

 Audio demonstration and practice tracks are included for select lines of music. Look for the audio icon throughout this book.

 Video demonstrations of exercises and key skills are included. Look for the video icon throughout this book.

 Supplemental content and additional repertoire for practice and reinforcement are available to download at the *SI Online* website below.

Visit the *SI Online* resource site to stay up to date with newly added content.
alfred.com/CreativeWarmUps

 Alfred Music
P.O. Box 10003
Van Nuys, CA 91410-0003
alfred.com

Copyright © 2017 by Alfred Music
All rights reserved. Printed in USA.

ISBN-10: 1-4706-3869-X (Book & Online Media)
ISBN-13: 978-1-4706-3869-6 (Book & Online Media)

MW01092301

Level 1: Sound Intonation
C Major

1

INTERVALS IN C MAJOR—*Listen for the interval that occurs at each fermata. Adjust to remove any "beats" in the sound. An interval is the distance from a root (first note) pitch to another pitch. Intervals in this exercise include a Major 2nd, Major 3rd, Perfect 4th, Perfect 5th, Major 6th, Major 7th, and Perfect 8th/Octave. Evaluate and refine your performance. Write out each interval starting on C using music notation. Switch parts on the repeat.*

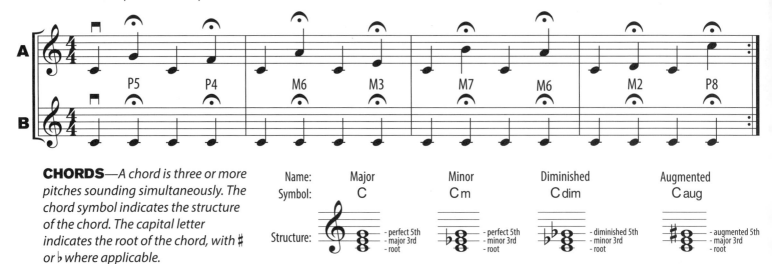

CHORDS—*A chord is three or more pitches sounding simultaneously. The chord symbol indicates the structure of the chord. The capital letter indicates the root of the chord, with ♯ or ♭ where applicable.*

Name:	Major	Minor	Diminished	Augmented
Symbol:	C	Cm	C dim	C aug
Structure:	- perfect 5th, - major 3rd, - root	- perfect 5th, - minor 3rd, - root	- diminished 5th, - minor 3rd, - root	- augmented 5th, - major 3rd, - root

Compare and contrast the chord symbols and structure of the various chords. Apply the same formulas using different roots.

2

MOVING CHORD TONES IN C MAJOR—*Listen to each C major chord and analyze which part of the chord (root, third, fifth, or octave) you are playing. Switch parts on the repeat.*

3

LAYERED TUNING AND BALANCE IN C MAJOR—*Listen, evaluate, and adjust the balance (relative volume of each instrument) and intonation as you enter. Switch parts on the repeat.*

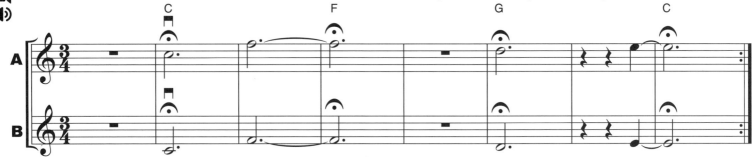

4

DIATONIC (SCALE) HARMONY IN C MAJOR—*Listen for the harmony (chord) that occurs at each fermata. Compare and contrast the difference between major and minor chords. Analyze whether you are playing the root, third, fifth, or octave in each chord. Switch parts on the repeat.*

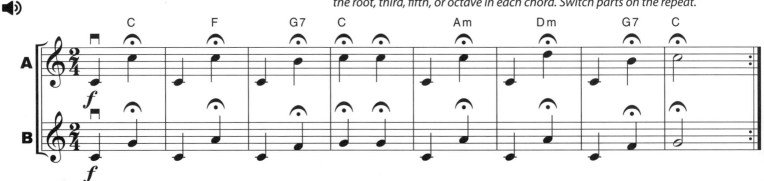

* The audio tracks for each exercise in Level 1 are a combination of all the string parts. Play along with the tracks to practice and refine your intonation.

5 **SHIFTING CHORD QUALITIES IN C MAJOR**—*Expressively perform each new chord and demonstrate how the triad changes. Triads (chords) will change from major to minor to diminished as they descend and then from minor to major to augmented as they ascend. ✖ before a note indicates a double sharp. Switch parts on the repeat.*

Play 3x

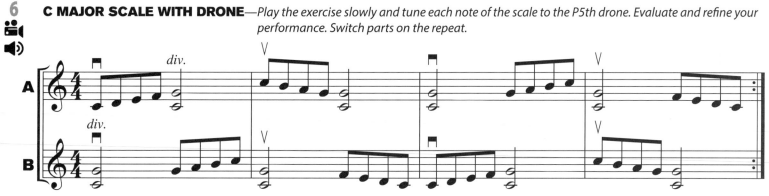

6 **C MAJOR SCALE WITH DRONE**—*Play the exercise slowly and tune each note of the scale to the P5th drone. Evaluate and refine your performance. Switch parts on the repeat.*

7 **C CHROMATIC SCALE WITH DRONE**—*Play slowly and tune each note of the scale to the C drone. Apply criteria to evaluate your performance as developed with your teacher. Switch parts on the repeat.*

8 **CHORALE IN C MAJOR**—*Expressively perform the chorale while listening to, evaluating, and adjusting each note to improve intonation. Identify intervals and listen for the chord (triad) character of each note. Respond to the question, "How do we judge the quality of musical works?"*

Harmonized by Johann Sebastian Bach
BWV 255

Largo (♩ = 60)

G Major

9 **INTERVALS IN G MAJOR**—*Listen for the interval that occurs at each fermata. Adjust to remove any "beats" in the sound. Intervals in this exercise include a Major 2nd, Major 3rd, Perfect 4th, Perfect 5th, Major 6th, Major 7th, and Perfect 8th/Octave. Evaluate and refine your performance. Write out each interval starting on G using music notation. Switch parts on the repeat.*

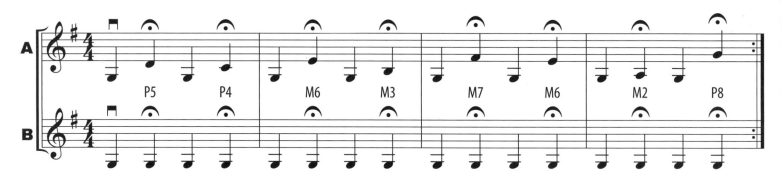

10 **MOVING CHORD TONES IN G MAJOR**—*Listen to each G major chord and analyze which part of the chord (root, third, fifth, or octave) you are playing. Switch parts on the repeat.*

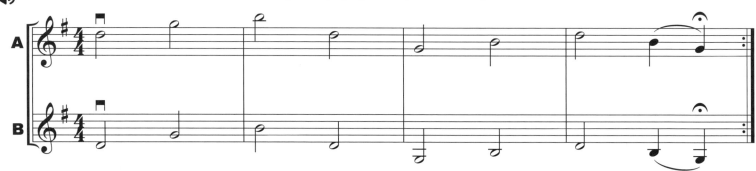

11 **LAYERED TUNING AND BALANCE IN G MAJOR**—*Listen, evaluate, and adjust the balance (relative volume between each instrument) and intonation as you enter. Switch parts on the repeat.*

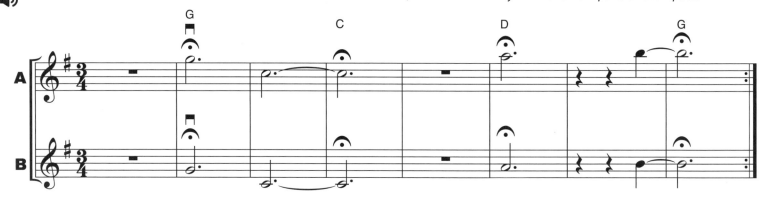

12 **DIATONIC (SCALE) HARMONY IN G MAJOR**—*Listen for the harmony (chord) that occurs at each fermata. Compare and contrast the difference between major and minor chords. Analyze whether you are playing the root, third, fifth, or octave in each chord. Switch parts on the repeat.*

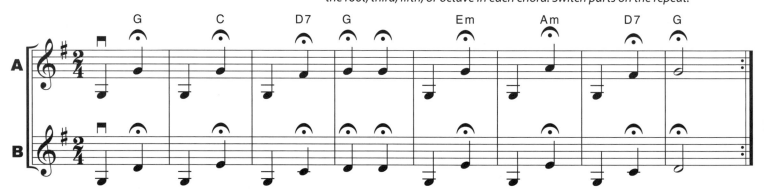

13 SHIFTING CHORD QUALITIES IN G MAJOR—*Expressively perform each new chord and demonstrate how the triad changes. Triads (chords) will change from major to minor to diminished as they descend and then from minor to major to augmented as they ascend. Switch parts on the repeat.*

Play 3x

14 G MAJOR SCALE WITH DRONE—*Play the exercise slowly and tune each note of the scale to the P5th drone. Evaluate and refine your performance. Switch parts on the repeat.*

15 G CHROMATIC SCALE WITH DRONE—*Play slowly and tune each note of the scale to the G drone. Apply criteria to evaluate your performance as developed with your teacher. Switch parts on the repeat.*

16 CHORALE IN G MAJOR—*Expressively perform the chorale while listening to, evaluating, and adjusting each note to improve intonation. Identify intervals and listen for the chord (triad) character of each note. Respond to the question, "How do we judge the quality of musical works?"*

Harmonized by Johann Sebastian Bach
BWV 281

D Major

17 **INTERVALS IN D MAJOR**—*Listen for the interval that occurs at each fermata. Adjust to remove any "beats" in the sound. Intervals in this exercise include a Major 2nd, Major 3rd, Perfect 4th, Perfect 5th, Major 6th, Major 7th, and Perfect 8th/Octave. Evaluate and refine your performance. Write out each interval starting on D using music notation. Switch parts on the repeat.*

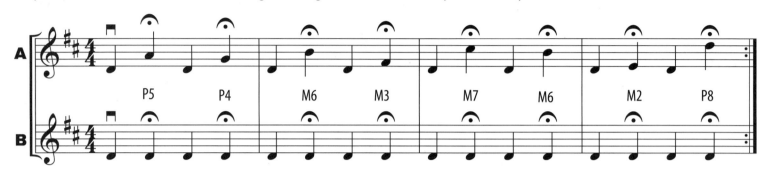

18 **MOVING CHORD TONES IN D MAJOR**—*Listen to each D major chord and analyze which part of the chord (root, third, fifth, or octave) you are playing. Switch parts on the repeat.*

19 **LAYERED TUNING AND BALANCE IN D MAJOR**—*Listen, evaluate, and adjust the balance (relative volume of each instrument) and intonation as you enter. Switch parts on the repeat.*

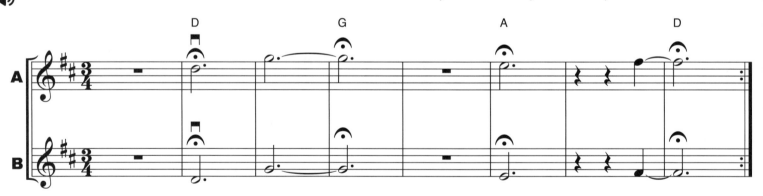

20 **DIATONIC (SCALE) HARMONY IN D MAJOR**—*Listen for the harmony (chord) that occurs at each fermata. Compare and contrast the difference between major and minor chords. Analyze whether you are playing the root, third, fifth, or octave in each chord. Switch parts on the repeat.*

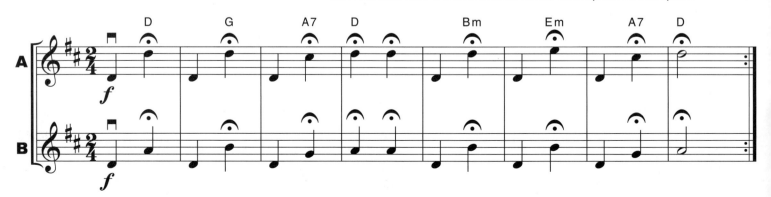

21 SHIFTING CHORD QUALITIES IN D MAJOR—*Expressively perform each new chord and demonstrate how the triad changes. Chords (triads) will change from major to minor to diminished as they descend and then from minor to major to augmented as they ascend. Switch parts on the repeat.*

Play 3x

22 D MAJOR SCALE WITH DRONE—*Play the exercise slowly and tune each note of the scale to the P5th drone. Evaluate and refine your performance. Switch parts on the repeat.*

23 D CHROMATIC SCALE WITH DRONE—*Play slowly and tune each note of the scale to the D drone. Apply criteria to evaluate your performance as developed with your teacher. Switch parts on the repeat.*

24 CHORALE IN D MAJOR—*Expressively perform the chorale while listening to, evaluating, and adjusting each note to improve intonation. Identify intervals and listen for the chord (triad) character of each note. Respond to the question, "How do we judge the quality of musical works?"*

Harmonized by Johann Sebastian Bach
BWV 327

A Major

25 **INTERVALS IN A MAJOR**—*Listen for the interval that occurs at each fermata. Adjust to remove any "beats" in the sound. Intervals in this exercise include a Major 2nd, Major 3rd, Perfect 4th, Perfect 5th, Major 6th, Major 7th, and Perfect 8th/Octave. Evaluate and refine your performance. Write out each interval starting on A using music notation. Switch parts on the repeat.*

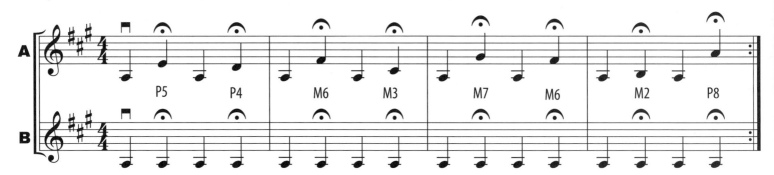

26 **MOVING CHORD TONES IN A MAJOR**—*Listen to each A major chord and analyze which part of the chord (root, third, fifth, or octave) you are playing. Switch parts on the repeat.*

27 **LAYERED TUNING AND BALANCE IN A MAJOR**—*Listen, evaluate, and adjust the balance (relative volume of each instrument) and intonation as you enter. Switch parts on the repeat.*

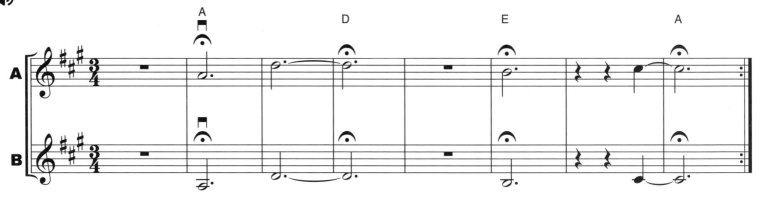

28 **DIATONIC (SCALE) HARMONY IN A MAJOR**—*Listen for the harmony (chord) that occurs at each fermata. Compare and contrast the difference between major and minor chords. Analyze whether you are playing the root, third, fifth, or octave in each chord. Switch parts on the repeat.*

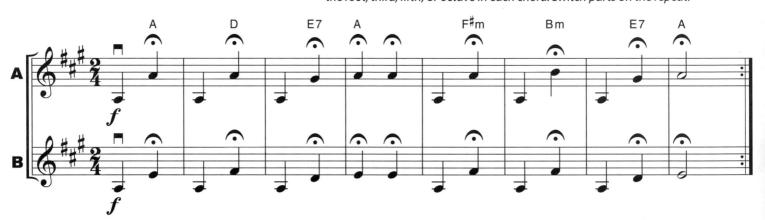

29 **SHIFTING CHORD QUALITIES IN A MAJOR**—*Expressively perform each new chord and demonstrate how the triad changes. Chords (triads) will change from major to minor to diminished as they descend and then from minor to major to augmented as they ascend. Switch parts on the repeat.*

Play 3x

30 **A MAJOR SCALE WITH DRONE**—*Play the exercise slowly and tune each note of the scale to the P5th drone. Evaluate and refine your performance. Switch parts on the repeat.*

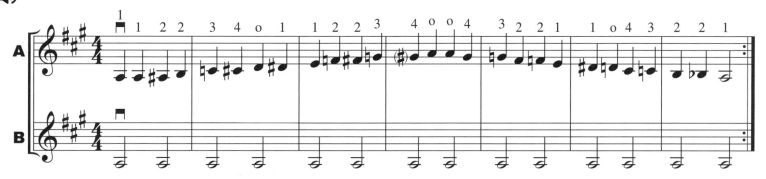

31 **A CHROMATIC SCALE WITH DRONE**—*Play slowly and tune each note of the scale to the A drone. Apply criteria to evaluate your performance as developed with your teacher. Switch parts on the repeat.*

32 **CHORALE IN A MAJOR**—*Expressively perform the chorale while listening to, evaluating, and adjusting each note to improve intonation. Identify intervals and listen for the chord (triad) character of each note. Respond to the question, "How do we judge the quality of musical works?"*

Harmonized by Johann Sebastian Bach
BWV 318

Largo (♩ = 60)

G Harmonic Minor

33 **INTERVALS IN G HARMONIC MINOR**—*Listen for the interval that occurs at each fermata. Adjust to remove any "beats" in the sound. Intervals in this exercise include a Major 2nd, Minor 3rd, Perfect 4th, Perfect 5th, Minor 6th, Major 7th, and Perfect 8th/Octave. Evaluate and refine your performance. Write out each interval starting on G using music notation. Switch parts on the repeat.*

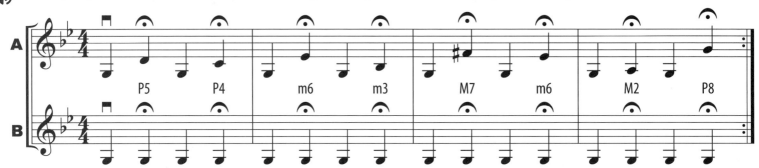

34 **MOVING CHORD TONES IN G HARMONIC MINOR**—*Listen to each G minor chord and analyze which part of the chord (root, third, fifth, or octave) you are playing. Switch parts on the repeat.*

35 **LAYERED TUNING AND BALANCE IN G HARMONIC MINOR**—*Listen, evaluate, and adjust the balance (relative volume of each instrument) and intonation as you enter. Switch parts on the repeat.*

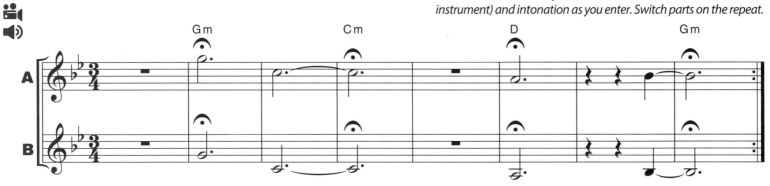

36 **DIATONIC (SCALE) HARMONY IN G HARMONIC MINOR**—*Listen for the harmony (chord) that occurs at each fermata. Compare and contrast the difference between major and minor chords. Analyze whether you are playing the root, third, fifth, or octave in each chord. Switch parts on the repeat.*

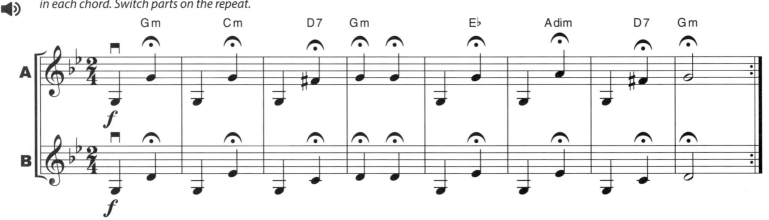

37 **G HARMONIC MINOR SCALE WITH DRONE**—*Play the exercise slowly and tune each note of the scale to the P5th drone. Evaluate and refine your performance. Switch parts on the repeat.*

38 **G CHROMATIC SCALE WITH DRONE**—*Play slowly and tune each note of the scale to the G drone. Apply criteria to evaluate your performance as developed with your teacher. Switch parts on the repeat.*

39 **CHORALE IN G MINOR**—*Expressively perform the chorale while listening to, evaluating, and adjusting each note to improve intonation. Identify intervals and listen for the chord (triad) character of each note. Respond to the question, "How do we judge the quality of musical works?"*

Harmonized by Johann Sebastian Bach
BWV 273

D Harmonic Minor

40 **INTERVALS IN D HARMONIC MINOR**—*Listen for the interval that occurs at each fermata. Adjust to remove any "beats" in the sound. Intervals in this exercise include a Major 2nd, Minor 3rd, Perfect 4th, Perfect 5th, Minor 6th, Major 7th, and Perfect 8th/Octave. Evaluate and refine your performance. Write out each interval starting on D using music notation. Switch parts on the repeat.*

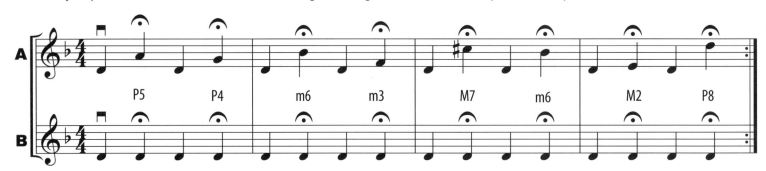

41 **MOVING CHORD TONES IN D HARMONIC MINOR**—*Listen to each D minor chord and analyze which part of the chord (root, third, fifth, or octave) you are playing. Switch parts on the repeat.*

42 **LAYERED TUNING AND BALANCE IN D HARMONIC MINOR**—*Listen, evaluate, and adjust the balance (relative volume of each instrument) and intonation as you enter. Switch parts on the repeat.*

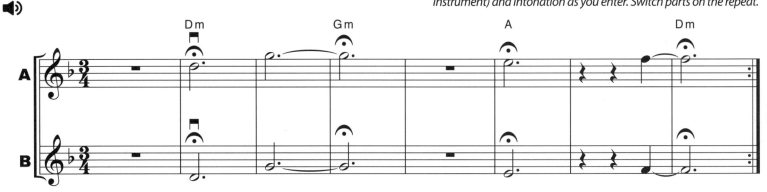

43 **DIATONIC (SCALE) HARMONY IN D HARMONIC MINOR**—*Listen for the harmony (chord) that occurs at each fermata. Compare and contrast the difference between major and minor chords. Analyze whether you are playing the root, third, fifth, or octave in each chord. Switch parts on the repeat.*

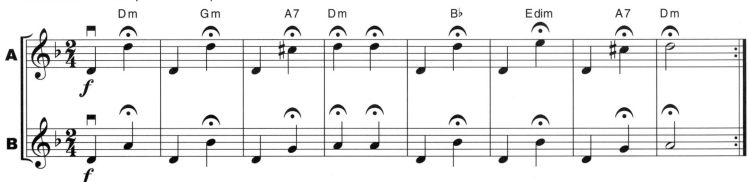

44 D HARMONIC MINOR SCALE WITH DRONE—*Play the exercise slowly and tune each note of the scale to the P5th drone. Evaluate and refine your performance. Switch parts on the repeat.*

45 D CHROMATIC SCALE WITH DRONE—*Play slowly and tune each note of the scale to the D drone. Apply criteria to evaluate your performance as developed with your teacher. Switch parts on the repeat.*

46 CHORALE IN D MINOR—*Expressively perform the chorale while listening to, evaluating, and adjusting each note to improve intonation. Identify intervals and listen for the chord (triad) character of each note. Respond to the question, "How do we judge the quality of musical works?"*

Harmonized by Johann Sebastian Bach
BWV 272

14

A Harmonic Minor

47 **INTERVALS IN A HARMONIC MINOR**—*Listen for the interval that occurs at each fermata. Adjust to remove any "beats" in the sound. Intervals in this exercise include a Major 2nd, Minor 3rd, Perfect 4th, Perfect 5th, Minor 6th, Major 7th, and Perfect 8th/Octave. Evaluate and refine your performance. Write out each interval starting on A using music notation. Switch parts on the repeat.*

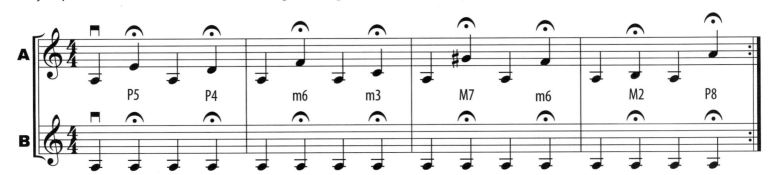

48 **MOVING CHORD TONES IN A HARMONIC MINOR**—*Listen to each A minor chord and analyze which part of the chord (root, third, fifth, or octave) you are playing. Switch parts on the repeat.*

49 **LAYERED TUNING AND BALANCE IN A HARMONIC MINOR**—*Listen, evaluate, and adjust the balance (relative volume of each instrument) and intonation as you enter. Switch parts on the repeat.*

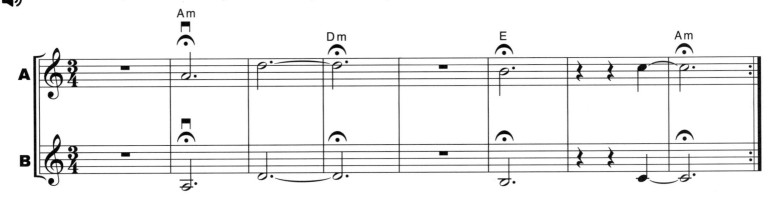

50 **DIATONIC (SCALE) HARMONY IN A HARMONIC MINOR**—*Listen for the harmony (chord) that occurs at each fermata. Compare and contrast the difference between major and minor chords. Analyze whether you are playing the root, third, fifth, or octave in each chord. Switch parts on the repeat.*

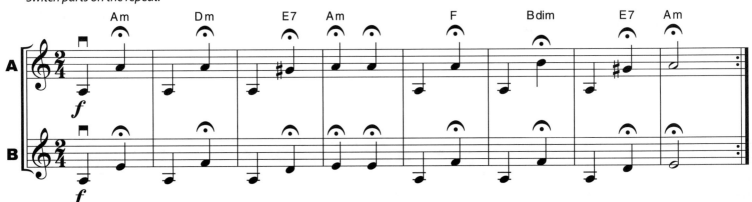

51 🔊 **A HARMONIC MINOR SCALE WITH DRONE**—*Play the exercise slowly and tune each note of the scale to the P5th drone. Evaluate and refine your performance. Switch parts on the repeat.*

52 🔊 **A CHROMATIC SCALE WITH DRONE**—*Play slowly and tune each note of the scale to the A drone. Apply criteria to evaluate your performance as developed with your teacher. Switch parts on the repeat.*

53 🔊 **CHORALE IN A MINOR**—*Expressively perform the chorale while listening to, evaluating, and adjusting each note to improve intonation. Identify intervals and listen for the chord (triad) character of each note. Respond to the question, "How do we judge the quality of musical works?"*

Harmonized by Johann Sebastian Bach
BWV 258

Largo (♩ = 60)

16

E Harmonic Minor

54 **INTERVALS IN E HARMONIC MINOR**—*Listen for the interval that occurs at each fermata. Adjust to remove any "beats" in the sound. Intervals in this exercise include a Major 2nd, Minor 3rd, Perfect 4th, Perfect 5th, Minor 6th, Major 7th, and Perfect 8th/Octave. Evaluate and refine your performance. Write out each interval starting on E using music notation. Switch parts on the repeat.*

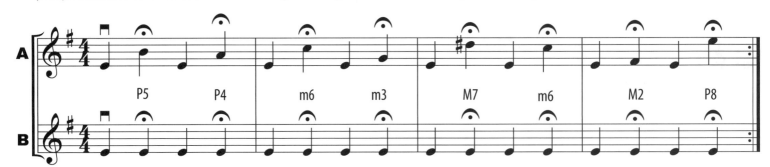

55 **MOVING CHORD TONES IN E HARMONIC MINOR**—*Listen to each E minor chord and analyze which part of the chord (root, third, fifth, or octave) you are playing. Switch parts on the repeat.*

56 **LAYERED TUNING AND BALANCE IN E HARMONIC MINOR**—*Listen, evaluate, and adjust the balance (relative volume of each instrument) and intonation as you enter. Switch parts on the repeat.*

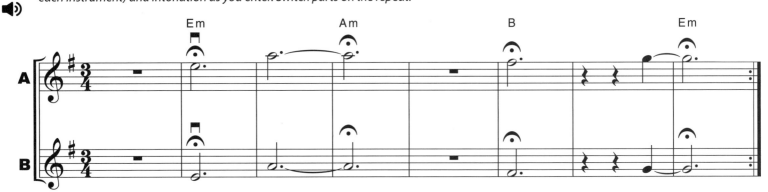

57 **DIATONIC (SCALE) HARMONY IN E HARMONIC MINOR**—*Listen for the harmony (chord) that occurs at each fermata. Compare and contrast the difference between major and minor chords. Analyze whether you are playing the root, third, fifth, or octave in each chord. Switch parts on the repeat.*

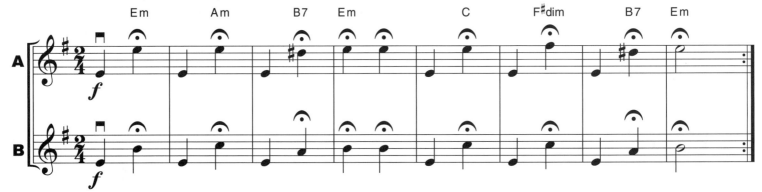

16

58 **E HARMONIC MINOR SCALE WITH DRONE**—*Play the exercise slowly and tune each note of the scale to the P5th drone. Evaluate and refine your performance. Switch parts on the repeat.*

59 **E CHROMATIC SCALE WITH DRONE**—*Play slowly and tune each note of the scale to the E drone. Apply criteria to evaluate your performance as developed with your teacher. Switch parts on the repeat.*

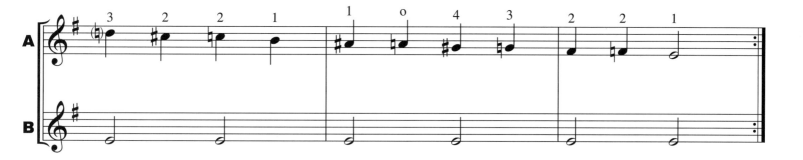

60 **CHORALE IN E MINOR**—*Expressively perform the chorale while listening to, evaluating, and adjusting each note to improve intonation. Identify intervals and listen for the chord (triad) character of each note. Respond to the question, "How do we judge the quality of musical works?"*

Harmonized by Johann Sebastian Bach
BWV 324

Extended Hand Positions

EXTENDED HAND POSITIONS—Violins/violas learn to play raised 3rd and lowered 1st & 4th fingers, cellos learn to play forward and backward extensions. Basses review 1st and ½ positions.

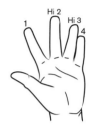

EXTENDED HAND POSITION (HIGHER)—Place your left-hand 1st finger in 1st position with a whole step between your 1st & 2nd finger and a half step between your 2nd & 3rd finger. Extend your 3rd finger up a half step while leaving your left-hand thumb in the same place. There will now be whole steps between your 1st & 2nd fingers and your 2nd & 3rd fingers.

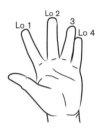

EXTENDED HAND POSITION (LOWER)—Place your left-hand 1st finger in 1st position with a half step between your 1st & 2nd finger and a whole step between your 2nd & 3rd finger. Extend your 1st finger down a half step while leaving your left-hand thumb in the same place. There will now be a whole step between your 1st & 2nd fingers and a whole step between your 2nd & 3rd fingers.

61 **PLAYING G♯ ON THE D STRING**—*Violins/violas play Hi 3 or Low 4, cellos play forward extension while basses play in 1st and ½ positions.*

62 **PLAYING E♭ ON THE D STRING**—*Violins/violas play Low 1, cellos play backward extension while basses play in 1st and ½ positions.*

63 **PLAYING C♯ ON THE G STRING**—*Violins/violas play Hi 3 or Low 4, cellos play forward extension while basses play in 1st and ½ positions.*

64 **PLAYING B♭ ON THE A STRING**—*Violins/violas play Low 1, cellos play backward extension while basses play in 1st and ½ positions.*

65 **EXTENDED HAND FRAMES NO. 1**—*Violins, violas, and cellos learn extended hand frames. Basses practice moving between 1st and ½ positions.*

66 **EXTENDED HAND FRAMES NO. 2**—*Violins, violas, and cellos learn extended hand frames. Basses practice moving between 1st and ½ positions.*

67 **EXTENDED HAND FRAMES NO. 3**—*Violins, violas, and cellos learn extended hand frames in 3rd position. Basses practice moving between 1st and ½ positions.*

68 **EXTENDED HAND FRAMES NO. 4**—*Violins, violas, and cellos learn extended hand frames in 4th position. Basses practice moving between 1st and ½ positions.*

Level 2: Sound Rhythms
Sound Rhythms in 4/4
Whole notes/rests, half notes/rests, quarter notes/rests, eighth notes/rests

Musicians use different systems to teach, learn, and practice rhythm patterns. Some systems, such as Counting, are based on counting the beats and their divisions and elongations. Other systems, such as Gordon and Takadimi, are based on how music feels and functions. In the drone examples, Counting, Gordon, and Takadimi systems are shown, and your teacher will determine which system to use. When counting aloud, numbers in bold are spoken and numbers in grey are spoken silently.

4 = Four beats, pulses, or macro-beats to a measure.

4 = A quarter note receives one beat, pulse, or macro-beat.

A. PULSE/MACRO-BEAT DRONE
Quarter notes are the unit of pulse in 4/4 time.

Counting	1	2	3	4
Gordon	Du	du	du	du
Takadimi	Ta	ta	ta	ta

B. SUBDIVISION/MICRO-BEAT DRONE
Eighth notes are the unit of subdivision in 4/4 time.

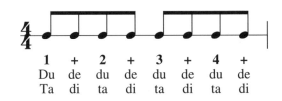

Counting	1	+	2	+	3	+	4	+
Gordon	Du	de	du	de	du	de	du	de
Takadimi	Ta	di	ta	di	ta	di	ta	di

🔊 * **69–73**

69 **QUARTER NOTES AND RESTS**—*Say, clap, and play each two-bar pattern using the pitch, tempo, and dynamic given by your teacher while others play drone A or B. Play patterns A, B & C continuously as directed by your teacher.*

70 **HALF NOTES AND RESTS**—*Say, clap, and play each two-bar pattern using the pitch, tempo, and dynamic given by your teacher while others play drone A or B. Play patterns A, B & C in a three-part round as directed by your teacher.*

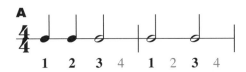

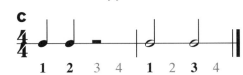

71 **WHOLE NOTES AND RESTS**—*Say, clap, and play each two-bar pattern using the pitch, tempo, and dynamic given by your teacher while others play drone A or B. Play patterns A, B & C while your stand partner plays patterns A, B & C from the previous line.*

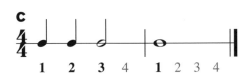

72 **EIGHTH NOTES AND RESTS**—*Say, clap, and play each two-bar pattern using the pitch, tempo, and dynamic given by your teacher while others play drone A or B. Play patterns A, B & C from the first four lines of the page continuously as directed by your teacher.*

73 **RHYTHM EVALUATION**—*Write in the rhythm syllables; then say, clap, and play the four-bar pattern using a pitch, tempo, and dynamic given by your teacher. Evaluate your performance using criteria developed with your teacher.*

Compose and notate new two-bar patterns using the rhythms above; then say, clap, and play them expressively.

---

* The audio track for each rhythm page in Level 2 consists of an extended drum pattern. Play along with the track to practice the rhythms on each page.

Sixteenth notes/rests

A. PULSE/MACRO-BEAT DRONE
Quarter notes are the unit of pulse in 4/4 time.

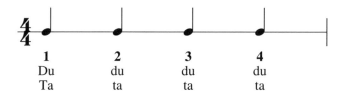

1	2	3	4
Du	du	du	du
Ta	ta	ta	ta

B. SUBDIVISION/MICRO-BEAT DRONE
Sixteenth notes are the unit of subdivision in 4/4 time.

1	e	+	a	2	e	+	a	3	e	+	a	4	e	+	a
Du	ta	de	ta	du	ta	de	ta	du	ta	de	ta	du	ta	de	ta
Ta	ka	di	mi	ta	ka	di	mi	ta	ka	di	mi	ta	ka	di	mi

🔊 **74–78**

74 **SIXTEENTH NOTES**—*Say, clap, and play each two-bar pattern using the pitch, tempo, and dynamic given by your teacher while others play drone A or B. Play patterns A & B continuously as directed by your teacher.*

A

1 2 3 + 4 +   1 e + a 2 e + a 3 + 4

B

1 e + a 2 + 3 e + a 4 +   1 e + a 2 e + a 3   4

75 **EIGHTH AND SIXTEENTH NOTES**—*Say, clap, and play each two-bar pattern using a pitch, tempo, and dynamic given by your teacher while others play drone A or B. Play patterns A & B in a two-part round as directed by your teacher.*

A

1 2 + 3 4 +   1 + a 2 + a 3 + a 4 + a

B

1 2 + 3 e + 4 e +   1 e + 2 e + a 3 e + 4 e + a

76 **SIXTEENTH NOTES AND EIGHTH RESTS**—*Say, clap, and play each two-bar pattern using a pitch, tempo, and dynamic given by your teacher while others play drone A or B. Play patterns A & B while your stand partner plays patterns A & B from the previous line.*

A

1 + 2 + a 3 + 4 + a   1 e + a 2 + a 3 e + 4 e + a

B

1 e + 2 e + 3 e + a 4 +   1 + a 2 + a 3   4 e + a

77 **SIXTEENTH NOTES AND RESTS**—*Say, clap, and play each two-bar pattern using a pitch, tempo, and dynamic given by your teacher while others play drone A or B. Play patterns A & B from the first four lines of the page continuously as directed by your teacher.*

A

1 e + a 2 e + a 3 e + a 4 e + a   1 e + a 2 + a 3 e + a 4 +

B

1 e + a 2 + 3 + a 4 + a   1 + 2 e + a 3 + 4 e + a

78 **RHYTHM EVALUATION**—*Write in the rhythm syllables; then say, clap, and play the four-bar pattern using a pitch, tempo, and dynamic given by your teacher. Evaluate your performance using criteria developed with your teacher.*

Compose and notate new two-bar patterns using the rhythms above; then say, clap, and play them expressively.

Dotted quarter notes/rests, dotted half notes/rests, dotted eighth notes/rests

A. PULSE/MACRO-BEAT DRONE
Quarter notes are the unit of pulse in 4/4 time.

B. SUBDIVISION/MICRO-BEAT DRONE
Eighth notes are the unit of subdivision in 4/4 time.

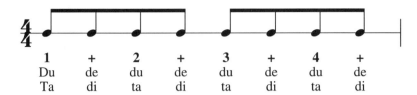

🔊 **79–83**

79 **DOTTED QUARTER NOTES**—*Say, clap, and play each two-bar pattern using a pitch, tempo, and dynamic given by your teacher while others play drone A or B. Play patterns A, B & C continuously as directed by your teacher.*

80 **DOTTED HALF NOTES**—*Say, clap, and play each two-bar pattern using a pitch, tempo, and dynamic given by your teacher while others play drone A or B. Play patterns A, B & C in a three-part round as directed by your teacher.*

81 **DOTTED EIGHTH NOTES**—*Say, clap, and play each two-bar pattern using a pitch, tempo, and dynamic given by your teacher while others play drone A or B. Play patterns A, B & C while your stand partner plays patterns A, B & C from the previous line.*

82 **TIES**—*Say, clap, and play each two-bar pattern using a pitch, tempo, and dynamic given by your teacher while others play drone A or B. Play patterns A, B & C from the first four lines of the page continuously as directed by your teacher.*

83 **RHYTHM EVALUATION**—*Write in the rhythm syllables; then say, clap, and play the four-bar pattern using a pitch, tempo, and dynamic given by your teacher. Evaluate your performance using criteria developed with your teacher.*

Compose and notate new two-bar patterns using the rhythms above; then say, clap, and play them expressively.

Syncopation

A. PULSE/MACRO-BEAT DRONE
Quarter notes are the unit of pulse in 4/4 time.

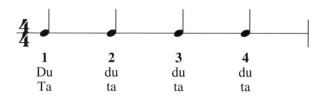

B. SUBDIVISION/MICRO-BEAT DRONE
Eighth notes are the unit of subdivision in 4/4 time.

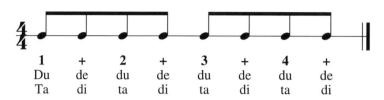

🔊 **84–88**

84 **QUARTER-/HALF-NOTE SYNCOPATION**—*Say, clap, and play each two-bar pattern using a pitch, tempo, and dynamic given by your teacher while others play drone A or B. Play patterns A, B & C continuously as directed by your teacher.*

85 **EIGHTH-/QUARTER-NOTE SYNCOPATION**—*Say, clap, and play each two-bar pattern using a pitch, tempo, and dynamic as directed by your teacher while others play drone A or B. Play patterns A, B & C in a three-part round as directed by your teacher.*

86 **SIXTEENTH-/EIGHTH-NOTE SYNCOPATION**—*Say, clap, and play each two-bar pattern using a pitch, tempo, and dynamic as directed by your teacher while others play drone A or B. Play patterns A & B while your stand partner plays patterns A & B from the previous line.*

87 **SYNCOPATION**—*Say, clap, and play each two-bar pattern using a pitch, tempo, and dynamic as directed by your teacher while others play drone A or B. Play patterns A, B & C from the first four lines of the page continuously as directed by your teacher.*

88 **RHYTHM EVALUATION**—*Write in the rhythm syllables; then say, clap, and play the four-bar pattern using a pitch, tempo, and dynamic given by your teacher. Evaluate your performance using criteria developed with your teacher.*

Compose and notate new two-bar patterns using the rhythms above; then say, clap, and play them expressively.

Sound Rhythms in Slow ¾ (counting in 3)

Dotted half notes/rests, half notes/rests, quarter notes/rests, eighth notes/rests

3 = Three beats, pulses, or macro-beats to a measure.

4 = A quarter note receives one beat, pulse, or macro-beat.

A. PULSE/MACRO-BEAT DRONE
Quarter notes are the unit of pulse in ¾ time.

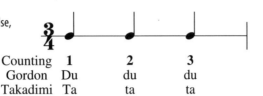

Counting	1	2	3
Gordon	Du	du	du
Takadimi	Ta	ta	ta

B. SUBDIVISION/MICRO-BEAT DRONE
Eighth notes are the unit of subdivision in ¾ time.

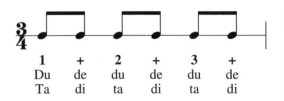

	1	+	2	+	3	+
	Du	de	du	de	du	de
	Ta	di	ta	di	ta	di

🔊 **89–93**

89 **QUARTER NOTES AND RESTS**—*Say, clap, and play each two-bar pattern using a pitch, tempo, and dynamic given by your teacher while others play drone A or B. Play patterns A, B & C continuously as directed by your teacher.*

A

B

C

90 **HALF NOTES, DOTTED HALF NOTES, AND RESTS**—*Say, clap, and play each two-bar pattern using a pitch, tempo, and dynamic given by your teacher while others play drone A or B. Play patterns A, B & C in a three-part round as directed by your teacher.*

A

B

C
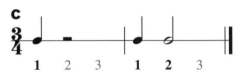

91 **EIGHTH NOTES AND RESTS**—*Say, clap, and play each two-bar pattern using a pitch, tempo, and dynamic given by your teacher while others play drone A or B. Play patterns A, B & C while your stand partner plays patterns A, B & C from the previous line.*

A

B
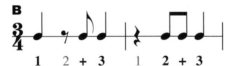

C

92 **DOTTED NOTES**—*Say, clap, and play each two-bar pattern using a pitch, tempo, and dynamic given by your teacher while others play drone A or B. Play patterns A, B & C from the first four lines of the page continuously as directed by your teacher.*

A

B

C
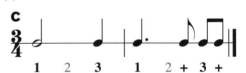

93 **RHYTHM EVALUATION**—*Write in the rhythm syllables; then say, clap, and play the six-bar pattern using a pitch, tempo, and dynamic given by your teacher. Evaluate your performance using criteria developed with your teacher.*

Compose and notate new two-bar patterns using the rhythms above; then say, clap, and play them expressively.

Sound Rhythms in Fast $\frac{3}{4}$ (counting in 1)

Dotted half notes/rests, half notes/rests, quarter notes/rests, eighth notes/rests

A. PULSE/MACRO-BEAT DRONE
Dotted half notes are the unit of pulse in fast $\frac{3}{4}$ time.

1
Du
Ta

B. SUBDIVISION/MICRO-BEAT DRONE
Quarter notes are the unit of subdivision in fast $\frac{3}{4}$ time.

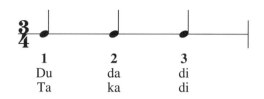

1   2   3
Du da di
Ta ka di

🔊 **94–98**

94 **DOTTED HALF NOTES/RESTS, HALF NOTES/RESTS, QUARTER NOTES/RESTS**—*Say, clap, and play each four-bar pattern using a pitch, tempo, and dynamic given by your teacher while others play drone A or B. Play patterns A & B continuously as directed by your teacher.*

95 **EIGHTH NOTES AND RESTS**—*Say, clap, and play each four-bar pattern using a pitch, tempo, and dynamic given by your teacher. Play patterns A & B in a two-part round as directed by your teacher.*

96 **DOTTED QUARTER NOTES AND RESTS**—*Say, clap, and play each four-bar pattern using a pitch, tempo, and dynamic given by your teacher while others play drone A or B. Play patterns A & B while your stand partner plays patterns A & B from the previous line.*

97 **HALF-/QUARTER-NOTE SYNCOPATION**—*Say, clap, and play each four-bar pattern using a pitch, tempo, and dynamic given by your teacher while others play drone A or B. Play patterns A & B from the first four lines of the page continuously as directed by your teacher.*

98 **RHYTHM EVALUATION**—*Write in the rhythm syllables; then say, clap, and play the six-bar pattern using a pitch, tempo, and dynamic given by your teacher. Evaluate your performance using criteria developed with your teacher.*

Compose and notate new two-bar patterns using the rhythms above; then say, clap, and play them expressively.

Sound Rhythms in 2/4

Half notes/rests, quarter notes/rests, eighth notes/rests, dotted quarter notes/rests

2 = Two beats, pulses, or macro-beats to a measure.

4 = A quarter note receives one beat, pulse, or macro-beat.

A. PULSE/MACRO-BEAT DRONE
Quarter notes are the unit of pulse in 2/4 time.

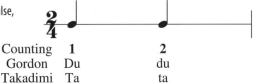

Counting	1	2
Gordon	Du	du
Takadimi	Ta	ta

B. SUBDIVISION/MICRO-BEAT DRONE
Eighth notes are the unit of subdivision in 2/4 time.

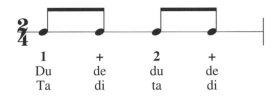

	1	+	2	+
	Du	de	du	de
	Ta	di	ta	di

🔊 **99–103**

99 **HALF NOTES/RESTS, QUARTER NOTES/RESTS**—*Say, clap, and play each four-bar pattern using a pitch, tempo, and dynamic given by your teacher while others play drone A or B. Play patterns A & B continuously as directed by your teacher.*

100 **EIGHTH NOTES AND RESTS**—*Say, clap, and play each four-bar pattern using a pitch, tempo, and dynamic given by your teacher while others play drone A or B. Play patterns A & B in a two-part round as directed by your teacher.*

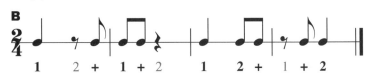

101 **DOTTED QUARTER NOTES AND RESTS**—*Say, clap, and play each four-bar pattern using a pitch, tempo, and dynamic given by your teacher while others play drone A or B. Play patterns A & B while your stand partner plays patterns A & B from the previous line.*

102 **EIGHTH-/QUARTER-NOTE SYNCOPATION**—*Say, clap, and play each four-bar pattern using a pitch, tempo, and dynamic given by your teacher while others play drone A or B. Play patterns A & B from the first four lines of the page continuously as directed by your teacher.*

103 **RHYTHM EVALUATION**—*Write in the rhythm syllables; then say, clap, and play the six-bar pattern using a pitch, tempo, and dynamic given by your teacher. Evaluate your performance using criteria developed with your teacher.*

Compose and notate new two-bar patterns using the rhythms above; then say, clap, and play them expressively.

Sound Rhythms in 2/2/¢ (cut-time)
Whole notes/rests, half notes/rests, quarter notes/rests

2 = Two beats, pulses, or macro-beats to a measure.

2 = A half note receives one beat, pulse, or macro-beat.

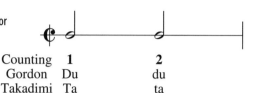

	A. PULSE/MACRO-BEAT DRONE	**B. SUBDIVISION/MICRO-BEAT DRONE**
	Half notes are the unit of pulse in cut time.	*Quarter notes are the unit of subdivision in cut time.*

Counting	**1**	**2**	**1**	**+**	**2**	**+**
Gordon	Du	du	Du	de	du	de
Takadimi	Ta	ta	Ta	di	ta	di

🔊 **104–108**

104 **WHOLE NOTES/RESTS, HALF NOTES/RESTS**—*Say, clap, and play each four-bar pattern using a pitch, tempo, and dynamic given by your teacher while others play drone A or B. Play patterns A & B continuously as directed by your teacher.*

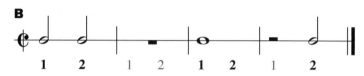

105 **QUARTER NOTES AND RESTS**—*Say, clap, and play each four-bar pattern using a pitch, tempo, and dynamic given by your teacher while others play drone A or B. Play patterns A & B in a two-part round as directed by your teacher.*

106 **DOTTED HALF NOTES AND RESTS**—*Say, clap, and play each four-bar pattern using a pitch, tempo, and dynamic given by your teacher while others play drone A or B. Play patterns A & B while your stand partner plays patterns A & B from the previous line.*

107 **QUARTER-NOTE SYNCOPATION**—*Say, clap, and play each four-bar pattern using a pitch, tempo, and dynamic given by your teacher while others play drone A or B. Play patterns A & B from the first four lines of the page continuously as directed by your teacher.*

108 **RHYTHM EVALUATION**—*Write in the rhythm syllables; then say, clap, and play the six-bar pattern using a pitch, tempo, and dynamic given by your teacher. Evaluate your performance using criteria developed with your teacher.*

Compose and notate new two-bar patterns using the rhythms above; then say, clap, and play them expressively.

Sound Rhythms in Slow $\frac{6}{8}$ (counting in 6)
Whole rests, dotted half notes, dotted quarter notes/rests, eighth notes/rests, dotted eighth notes

6 = Six beats, pulses, or macro-beats to a measure.
8 = An eighth note receives one beat, pulse, or macro-beat.

A. PULSE/MACRO-BEAT DRONE
Eighth notes are the unit of pulse in $\frac{6}{8}$ time.

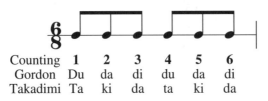

Counting	1	2	3	4	5	6
Gordon	Du	da	di	du	da	di
Takadimi	Ta	ki	da	ta	ki	da

B. SUBDIVISION/MICRO-BEAT DRONE
Sixteenth notes are the unit of subdivision in $\frac{6}{8}$ time.

	1	+	2	+	3	+	4	+	5	+	6	+
	Du	ta	da	ta	di	ta	du	ta	da	ta	di	ta
	Ta	va	ki	di	da	ma	ta	va	ki	di	da	ma

🔊 **109–113**

109 **EIGHTH NOTES, DOTTED QUARTER NOTES, DOTTED HALF NOTES, AND RESTS**—*Say, clap, and play each two-bar pattern using a pitch, tempo, and dynamic given by your teacher while others play drone A or B. Play patterns A, B & C continuously as directed by your teacher.*

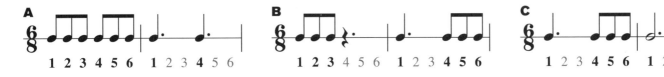

110 **DOTTED QUARTER NOTES, QUARTER NOTES, EIGHTH NOTES, AND RESTS**—*Say, clap, and play each two-bar pattern using a pitch, tempo, and dynamic given by your teacher while others play drone A or B. Play patterns A, B & C in a three-part round as directed by your teacher.*

111 **SIXTEENTH NOTES**—*Say, clap, and play each two-bar pattern using a pitch, tempo, and dynamic given by your teacher while others play drone A or B. Play patterns A, B & C while your stand partner plays patterns A, B & C from the previous line.*

112 **DOTTED EIGHTH NOTES**—*Say, clap, and play each two-bar pattern using a pitch, tempo, and dynamic given by your teacher while others play drone A or B. Play patterns A, B & C from the first four lines of the page continuously as directed by your teacher.*

113 **RHYTHM EVALUATION**—*Write in the rhythm syllables; then say, clap, and play the six-bar pattern using a pitch, tempo, and dynamic given by your teacher. Evaluate your performance using criteria developed with your teacher.*

Compose and notate new two-bar patterns using the rhythms above; then say, clap, and play them expressively.

Sound Rhythms in Fast ⁶⁄₈ (counting in 2)

Dotted half notes, dotted quarter notes/rests, eighth notes/rests, dotted eighth notes/rests

6 = Two beats, pulses, or macro-beats to a measure.

8 = A dotted quarter note receives one beat, pulse, or macro-beat.

A. PULSE/MACRO-BEAT DRONE
Dotted quarter notes are the unit of pulse in ⁶⁄₈ time.

Counting	1	4
Gordon	Du	du
Takadimi	Ta	ta

B. SUBDIVISION/MICRO-BEAT DRONE
Eighth notes are the unit of subdivision in ⁶⁄₈ time.

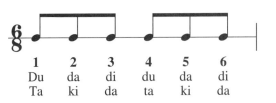

Counting	1	2	3	4	5	6
Gordon	Du	da	di	du	da	di
Takadimi	Ta	ki	da	ta	ki	da

🔊 **114–118**

114 EIGHTH NOTES, DOTTED QUARTER NOTES, DOTTED HALF NOTES, AND RESTS—*Say, clap, and play each two-bar pattern using a pitch, tempo, and dynamic given by your teacher while others play drone A or B. Play patterns A, B & C continuously as directed by your teacher.*

  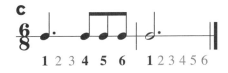

115 DOTTED QUARTER NOTES, QUARTER NOTES, EIGHTH NOTES, AND RESTS—*Say, clap, and play each two-bar pattern using a pitch, tempo, and dynamic given by your teacher while others play drone A or B. Play patterns A, B & C in a three-part round as directed by your teacher.*

116 DOTTED QUARTER NOTES, QUARTER NOTES, EIGHTH NOTES, AND SIXTEENTH NOTES—*Say, clap, and play each two-bar pattern using a pitch, tempo, and dynamic given by your teacher while others play drone A or B. Play patterns A, B & C while your stand partner plays patterns A, B & C from the previous line.*

117 DOTTED EIGHTH NOTES—*Say, clap, and play each two-bar pattern using a pitch, tempo, and dynamic given by your teacher while others play drone A or B. Play patterns A, B & C while your stand partner plays patterns A, B & C from the previous line.*

118 RHYTHM EVALUATION—*Write in the rhythm syllables; then say, clap, and play the six-bar pattern using a pitch, tempo, and dynamic given by your teacher. Evaluate your performance using criteria developed with your teacher.*

Compose and notate new two-bar patterns using the rhythms above; then say, clap, and play them expressively.

Level 3: Sound Bowing Fluency and Choreography
Bowing Lanes, Parts of the Bow, and Bow Distribution (play in various tempos)

BOWING LANES—Play all bowing fluency exercises in the mezzo-forte lane. To learn more about bowing lanes, weight, and speed see *Sound Innovations: Sound Development, Warm-up Exercises for Tone and Technique, Intermediate String Orchestra.*

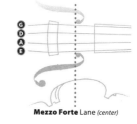

Mezzo Forte Lane *(center)*

PARTS OF THE BOW—The whole bow (WB) can be divided into two or three parts: the upper half (U2) and lower half (L2) or the lower third (L3), middle third (M3), and upper third (U3).

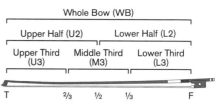

STARTING POINTS OF THE BOW—The bow can be placed on the string in five different starting points: the frog (F), lower third (⅓), middle (½), upper third (⅔), and tip (T).

BOW DISTRIBUTION—The process of planning ahead by adjusting bow speed, weight, and placement to be in the right part of the bow. Playing in the right part of the bow is crucial to a fluid bow stroke.

119 **PLACE THE BOW AT THE FROG, TIP, AND MIDDLE STARTING POINTS**—
Place the bow silently on the D string as indicated. Now go back and place it with your eyes closed. Open your eyes to evaluate the accuracy of your placement. Relax your right hand after each bow reset.

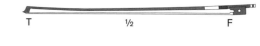

120 **PLACE THE BOW AT THE FROG, LOWER THIRD, AND MIDDLE STARTING POINTS**—*Place the bow silently on the D string as indicated. Now go back and place it with your eyes closed. Open your eyes to evaluate the accuracy of your placement. Relax your right hand after each bow reset.*

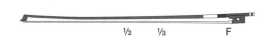

121 **PLACE THE BOW AT THE MIDDLE, UPPER THIRD, AND TIP STARTING POINTS**—*Place the bow silently on the D string as indicated. Now go back and place it with your eyes closed. Open your eyes to evaluate the accuracy of your placement. Relax your right hand after each bow reset.*

122 **PLACE THE BOW AT VARIOUS STARTING POINTS**—*Place the bow silently on the D string as indicated. Now go back and place it with your eyes closed. Open your eyes to evaluate the accuracy of your placement. Relax your right hand after each bow reset.*

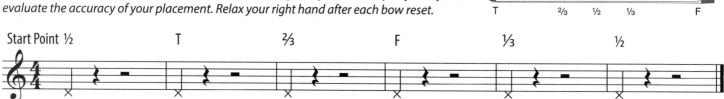

Playing in Different Parts of the Bow (play in various tempos)

Symmetrical, Even-Length Bowing Patterns (play in various tempos)

129 **SYMMETRICAL, SHORT-LENGTH BOWING IN THE MIDDLE THIRD OF THE BOW**—*Play* Boil Them Cabbage Down *in the middle third of the bow.*

130 **SYMMETRICAL, SHORT-LENGTH BOWING IN THE UPPER THIRD OF THE BOW**—*Play* Boil Them Cabbage Down *in the upper third of the bow.*

131 **SYMMETRICAL, SHORT-LENGTH BOWING IN THE LOWER THIRD OF THE BOW**—*Play* Boil Them Cabbage Down *in the lower third of the bow.*

132 **SYMMETRICAL, MEDIUM-LENGTH BOWING IN THE LOWER HALF OF THE BOW**—*Play* Boil Them Cabbage Down *in the lower half of the bow.*

133 **SYMMETRICAL, MEDIUM-LENGTH BOWING IN THE UPPER HALF OF THE BOW**—*Play* Boil Them Cabbage Down *in the upper half of the bow.*

134 **SYMMETRICAL, LONG-LENGTH BOWING USING THE WHOLE BOW**—*Play* Boil Them Cabbage Down *using the whole bow.*

Compare and contrast how the eighth-note exercises sound differently when played in different parts of the bow.

Asymmetrical, Long/Short-Length Bowing Patterns (play in various tempos)

135 **ASYMMETRICAL, LONG/SHORT-LENGTH BOWING IN THE MIDDLE THIRD OF THE BOW**—*Play* Finnegan's Wake *using a slower bow speed on the dotted eighth notes and a faster bow speed on the sixteenth notes. Each note will require the same amount of bow length.*

136 **ASYMMETRICAL, LONG/SHORT-LENGTH BOWING IN THE UPPER THIRD OF THE BOW**—*Play* Finnegan's Wake *using a slower bow speed on the dotted eighth notes and a faster bow speed on the sixteenth notes. Each note will require the same amount of bow length.*

137 **ASYMMETRICAL, LONG/SHORT-LENGTH BOWING IN THE LOWER THIRD OF THE BOW**—*Play* Finnegan's Wake *using a slower bow speed on the dotted eighth notes and a faster bow speed on the sixteenth notes. Each note will require the same amount of bow length.*

138 **ASYMMETRICAL, LONG/SHORT-LENGTH BOWING IN THE LOWER HALF OF THE BOW**—*Play* The Muffin Man *using a slower bow speed on the dotted quarter notes and a faster bow speed on the eighth notes.*

139 **ASYMMETRICAL, LONG/SHORT-LENGTH BOWING IN THE UPPER HALF OF THE BOW**—*Play* The Muffin Man *using a slower bow speed on the dotted quarter notes and a faster bow speed on the eighth notes.*

140 **ASYMMETRICAL, LONG/SHORT-LENGTH BOWING USING THE WHOLE BOW**—*Play* All Through The Night *using a slow bow speed on the dotted half notes and a fast bow speed on quarter notes.*

34

Symmetrical, Even-Length Bowing Patterns (play in various tempos)

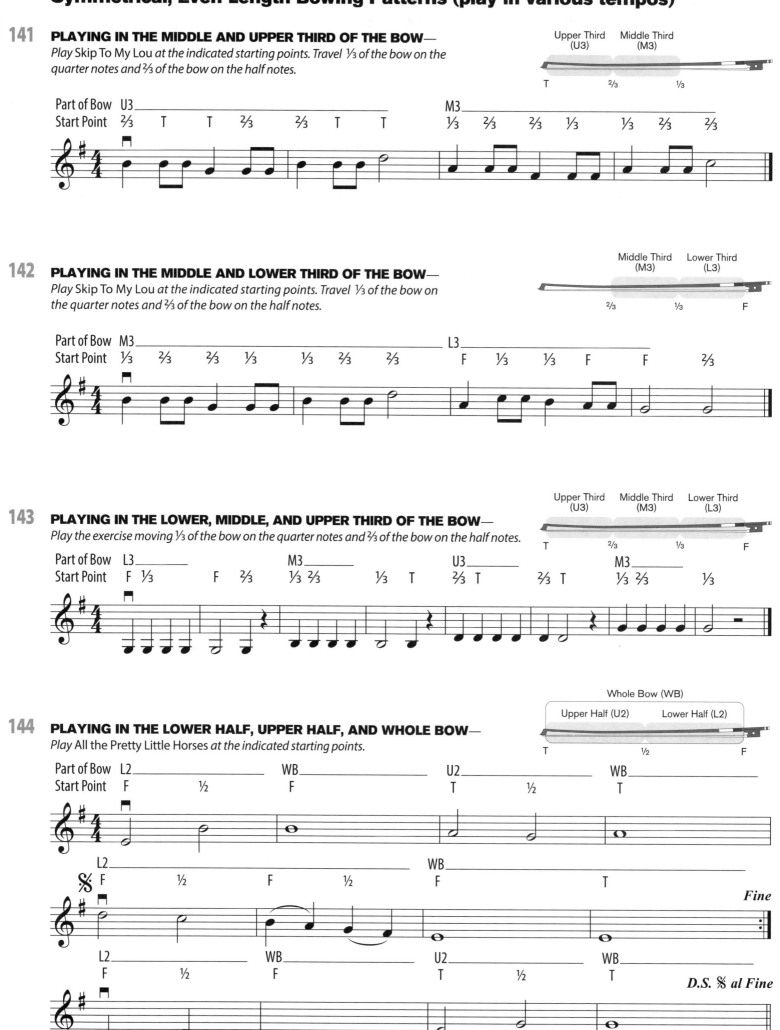

Engaging the Whole Arm, Forearm, Wrist, Hand, and Fingers (play in various tempos)

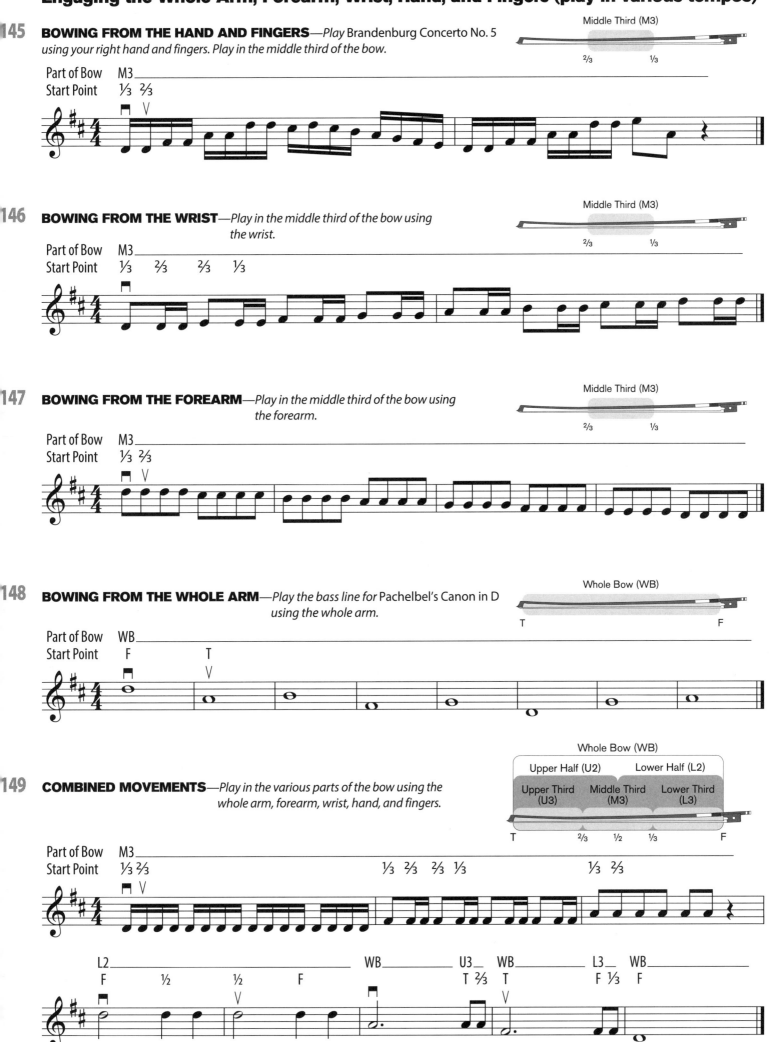

"Z Bowings" – Long/Short, Short Bowing Patterns (play in various tempos)

150 **"Z BOWINGS" IN A FAST TEMPO**—*Play "Praeludium" from* Holberg Suite *by Edvard Grieg in the middle third of the bow going from the ⅓ to ⅔ starting points.*

151 **"Z BOWINGS" IN A MODERATE TEMPO**—*Play* Humoreske *by Antonín Dvořák in the middle third of the bow. Move the bow slowly on the dotted eighth notes and quickly on the sixteenth notes.*

152 **"Z BOWINGS" IN A SLOW TEMPO**—*Play* Skye Boat Song *using the lower half, upper half, and whole bow.*

Slurs, Louré/Portato Bowings (play in various tempos)

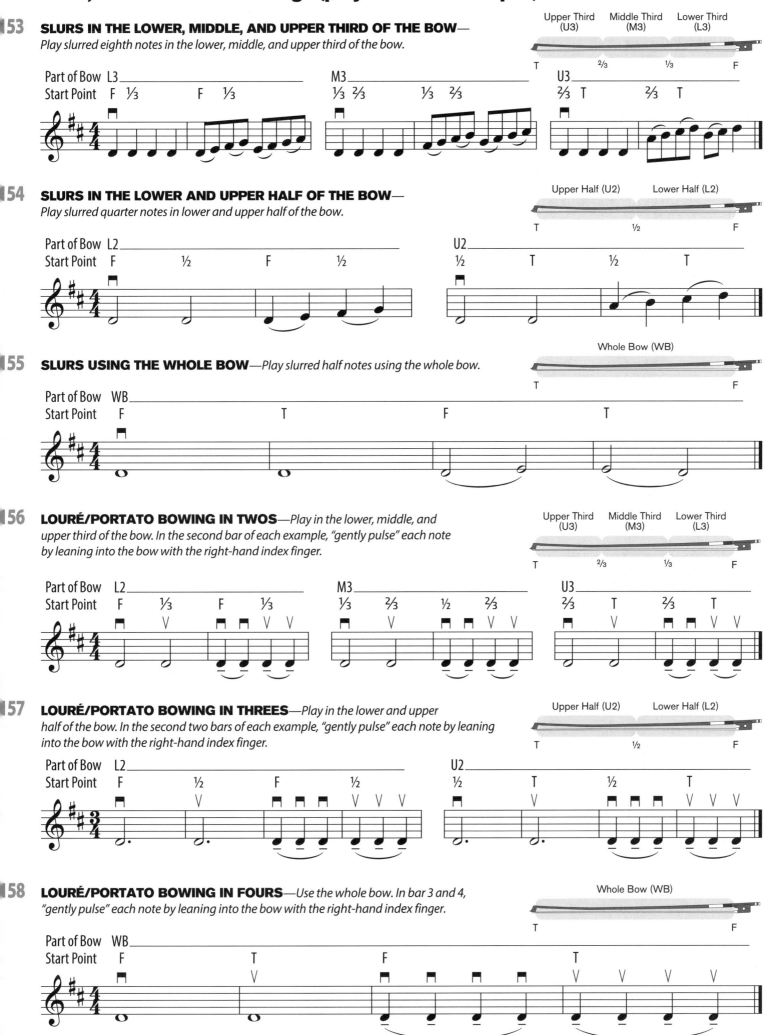

Hooked Bowings – Legato (play in various tempos)

159 **LEGATO HOOKED BOWING IN THE LOWER, MIDDLE, AND UPPER THIRD OF THE BOW IN 2/4**—*Play in the lower, middle, and upper third of the bow. In the second two bars of each example, "gently pulse" both notes by leaning into the bow with the right-hand index finger.*

160 **LEGATO HOOKED BOWING IN THE LOWER, MIDDLE, AND UPPER THIRD OF THE BOW IN 3/4**—*Play in the lower, middle, and upper third of the bow. In the second two bars of each example, "gently pulse" both notes by leaning into the bow with the right-hand index finger.*

161 **LEGATO HOOKED BOWING IN THE LOWER HALF AND UPPER HALF OF THE BOW IN 4/4**—*Play in the lower and upper half of the bow. In the second bar of each example, "gently pulse" all four notes by leaning into the bow with the right-hand index finger.*

162 **LEGATO HOOKED BOWING IN THE LOWER AND UPPER HALF OF THE BOW IN 6/8**—*Play in the lower and upper half of the bow. In the second bar of each example, "gently pulse" all four notes by leaning into the bow with the right-hand index finger.*

163 **LEGATO HOOKED BOWING USING THE WHOLE BOW IN 4/4**—*Play using the whole bow. In bar 3 and 4, "gently pulse" both notes by leaning into the bow with the right-hand index finger.*

164 **LEGATO HOOKED BOWING USING THE WHOLE BOW IN 6/8**—*Play using the whole bow. In bar 3 and 4, "gently pulse" both notes by leaning into the bow with the right-hand index finger.*

Hooked Bowings – Staccato (play in various tempos)

165 **STACCATO HOOKED BOWING IN THE LOWER, MIDDLE, AND UPPER THIRD OF THE BOW IN 2/4**—*Play in the lower, middle, and upper third of the bow. In the second two bars of each example, stop the bow between the dotted quarter and eighth notes.*

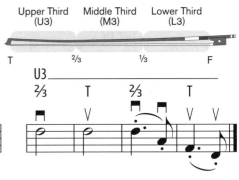

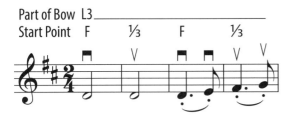 

166 **STACCATO HOOKED BOWING IN THE LOWER, MIDDLE, AND UPPER THIRD OF THE BOW IN 3/4**—*Play in the lower, middle, and upper third of the bow. In the second two bars of each example, stop the bow between the half and quarter notes.*

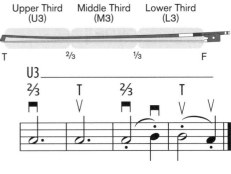

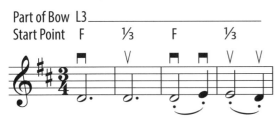 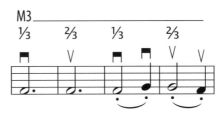

167 **STACCATO HOOKED BOWING IN THE LOWER AND UPPER HALF OF THE BOW IN 4/4**—*Play in the lower and upper half of the bow. In the second bar of each example, stop the bow between the dotted quarter and eighth notes.*

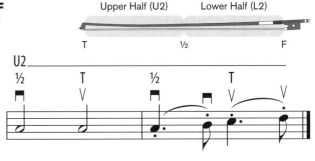

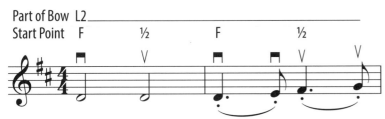

168 **STACCATO HOOKED BOWING IN THE LOWER AND UPPER HALF OF THE BOW IN 6/8**—*Play in the lower and upper half of the bow. In the second bar of each example, stop the bow between the quarter and eighth notes.*

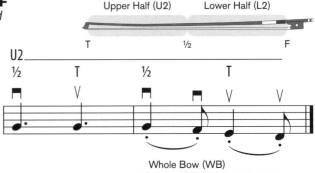

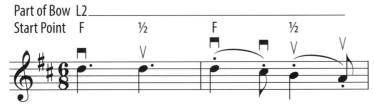

169 **STACCATO HOOKED BOWING USING THE WHOLE BOW IN 4/4**—*Play using the whole bow. In bar 3 and 4, stop the bow between the quarter notes.*

170 **STACCATO HOOKED BOWING USING THE WHOLE BOW IN 6/8**—*Play using the whole bow. In bar 3 and 4, stop the bow between the dotted quarter, quarter, and eighth notes.*

Two-String Crossings — violins and violas move from D up to A while cellos and basses move from D down to A (play in various tempos)

171 TWO-STRING CROSSINGS USING THE WHOLE BOW STARTING DOWN BOW—
Start down bow following the curve (⌒) of the bridge by lowering and raising the right arm.
(The upper arm starts the motion.)

172 TWO-STRING CROSSINGS USING THE WHOLE BOW STARTING UP BOW—
Start up bow moving opposite the curve (⌣) of the bridge by lowering and raising and the right arm.

173 TWO-STRING CROSSINGS IN THE LOWER HALF OF THE BOW
STARTING DOWN BOW—*Start down bow following the curve (⌒) of the bridge by lowering and raising the right arm and adding the wrist and fingers.*

174 TWO-STRING CROSSINGS IN THE LOWER HALF OF THE BOW
STARTING UP BOW—*Start up bow moving against the curve (⌣) of the bridge by lowering and raising the right arm and adding the wrist and fingers.*

175 TWO-STRING CROSSINGS IN THE UPPER HALF OF THE BOW
STARTING DOWN BOW—*Start down bow following the curve (⌒) of the bridge by lowering and raising the right arm and adding the wrist and fingers.*

176 TWO-STRING CROSSINGS IN THE UPPER HALF OF THE BOW
STARTING UP BOW—*Start up bow moving against the curve (⌣) of the bridge by lowering and raising the right arm and adding the wrist and fingers.*

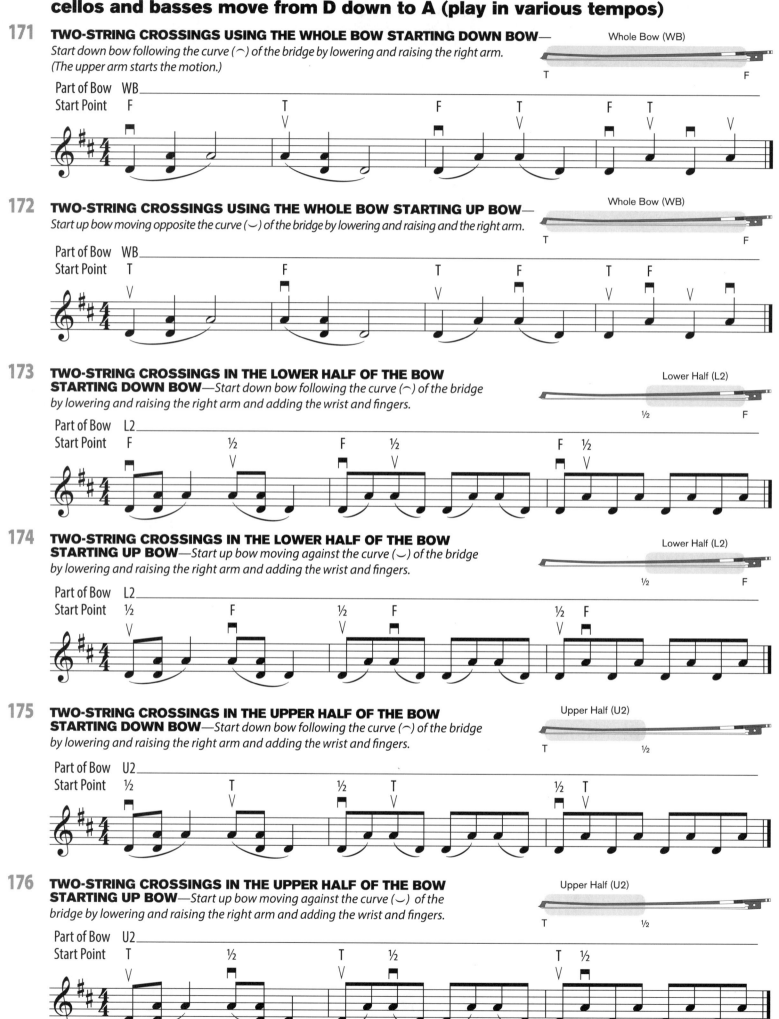

Two-String Crossings – violins and violas move from D up to A while cellos and basses move from D down to A (play in various tempos)

177 TWO-STRING CROSSINGS IN THE LOWER THIRD OF THE BOW—
Play the exercise following the curve (⌒) and then moving opposite to the curve (⌣) of the bridge using wrist and fingers.

178 TWO-STRING CROSSINGS IN THE MIDDLE THIRD OF THE BOW—
Play the exercise following the curve (⌒) and then moving opposite to the curve (⌣) of the bridge using wrist and fingers.

179 TWO-STRING CROSSINGS IN THE UPPER THIRD OF THE BOW—
Play the exercise following the curve (⌒) and then moving opposite to the curve (⌣) of the bridge using wrist and fingers.

180 TWO-STRING CROSSINGS AT THE 1/3 START POINT—
Cross strings using primarily the right-hand wrist and fingers.

181 TWO-STRING CROSSINGS AT THE 1/2 START POINT—
Cross strings using primarily the right-hand wrist and fingers.

182 TWO-STRING CROSSINGS AT THE 2/3 START POINT—
Cross strings using primarily the right-hand wrist and fingers.

Three-String Crossings — violins, violas play G-D-B, B-D-G, cellos, basses play B-D-B, B-D-B (play in various tempos)

183 **THREE-STRING CROSSINGS USING THE WHOLE BOW**—*Cross three strings by following the curve (⌢) of the bridge in the bars that start down bow, and move opposite the curve (⌣) of the bridge in the bars that start up bow.*

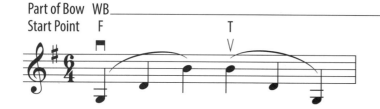

184 **THREE-STRING CROSSINGS IN THE LOWER THEN UPPER HALF OF THE BOW**—*Cross three strings by following the curve (⌢) of the bridge in the bars that start down bow, and move opposite the curve (⌣) of the bridge in the bars that start up bow.*

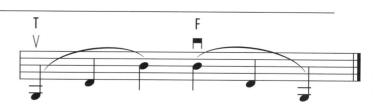

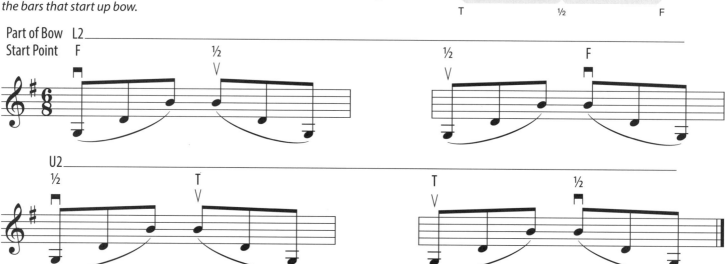

185 **THREE-STRING CROSSINGS IN THE LOWER, MIDDLE, AND UPPER THIRD OF THE BOW**—*Cross three strings by following the curve (⌢) of the bridge in the bars that start down bow, and move opposite the curve (⌣) of the bridge in the bars that start up bow.*

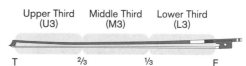

Four-String Crossings — violins play G-D-B-G, G-B-D-G, violas play D-G-D-B, B-D-G-D, cellos play B-D-B-D, D-B-D-B, basses play B-D-B-G, G-B-D-B (play in various tempos)

186 **FOUR-STRING CROSSINGS USING THE WHOLE BOW—**
Cross four strings by following the curve (⌢) of the bridge in the bars that start down bow, and move opposite the curve (⌣) of the bridge in the bars that start up bow.

187 **FOUR-STRING CROSSINGS IN THE LOWER HALF AND UPPER HALF OF THE BOW—***Cross four strings by following the curve (⌢) of the bridge in the bars that start down bow, and move opposite the curve (⌣) of the bridge in the bars that start up bow.*

188 **FOUR-STRING CROSSINGS IN THE LOWER THIRD, MIDDLE THIRD, AND UPPER THIRD OF THE BOW—***Cross four strings by following the curve (⌢) of the bridge in the bars that start down bow, and move opposite the curve (⌣) of the bridge in the bars that start up bow.*

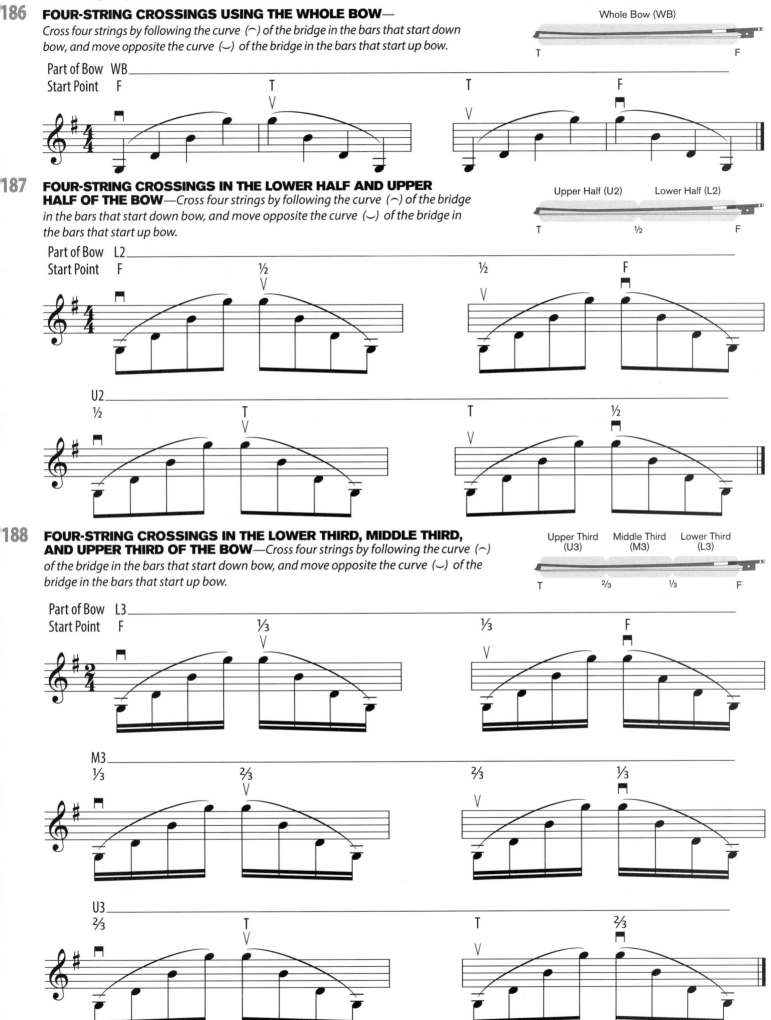

Level 4: Sound Creativity

Classical Chaconne

189 **A NATURAL MINOR (Aeolian) SCALE**—*Play the A natural minor scale.*

A HARMONIC MINOR SCALE—*Play the A harmonic minor scale.*

CHACONNE—The term chaconne (shä-'kòn) gained popularity in the 17th century and refers to musical variations over a repeated harmonic progression (similar in concept to the twelve-bar blues in jazz). In Claudio Monteverdi's madrigal *Lamento della Ninfa*, published in 1638, the repeated/ostinato bass line chromatically descends as an expression for sadness or lament. Interestingly, Monteverdi added performance notes encouraging the soprano soloist to sing according to her emotions while the accompanying trio performs the harmonies in strict tempo. Thus, every performance of this piece has a personal and unique rendition. As you play the Classical, Jazz, Latin, and Rock Chaconnes, strive to express emotions through the music. Respond to the question, "How can you make music convey emotions like fear, sadness, joy, surprise, and excitement?"

190 **CLASSICAL CHACONNE**—*Expressively perform* Classical Chaconne *based on Monteverdi's* Lamento della Ninfa *as directed by your teacher. At bar 13, create an improvised solo by using pitches from the A natural minor or A harmonic minor scale or by combining two-bar riffs from the rhythm and melodic riffs page.*

* The audio track for *Classical Chaconne* is an extended loop of bars 13–20. Practice improvising using the rhythm and melodic riffs on page 45.

Classical Chaconne Rhythm and Melodic Riffs

CLASSICAL RHYTHM RIFFS—*Echo back the rhythm riffs aurally or by reading on a pitch of your teacher's choice. Use the rhythm riffs to create a four- or eight-bar solo in bars 13–20 of the Classical Chaconne. Create and write your own rhythm riff in the blank measures.*

CLASSICAL MELODIC RIFFS—*Echo back the melodic riffs by reading or aurally as played by your teacher. Use the melodic riffs to create a four- or eight-bar solo in bars 13–20 of the Classical Chaconne. Create and write your own melodic riff in the blank measures.*

MELODIC RIFF BOWING/ARTICULATION VARIATIONS—*Echo back the melodic riff variations either by reading or aurally as played by your teacher. Each group of two bars has the same notes, but variations are created by adding new slurs, bowings, and articulations. Play line B to practice the rhythms that are created from the bowings in line A. Create and write your own bowing/articulation riff in the blank measures.*

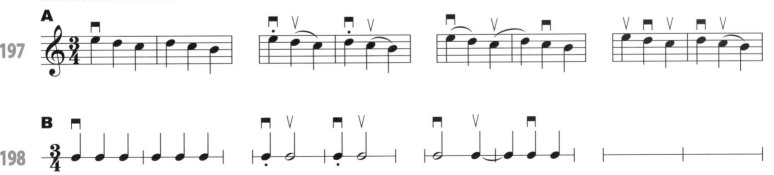

CREATIVITY ASSIGNMENT—*Play the rhythm and melodic riffs adding slurs, articulations, and different bowings as creative tools.*

Jazz Chaconne

199 **JAZZ CHACONNE**—*Expressively perform* Jazz Chaconne *as directed by your teacher. At bar 9, create an improvised solo by using pitches from the A natural minor or A harmonic minor scale, or by combining two-bar riffs from the rhythm and melodic riffs page. Compare and contrast the* Classical *and* Jazz Chaconne *discussing how their styles and genres differ. Discuss the periods and cultures they represent.*

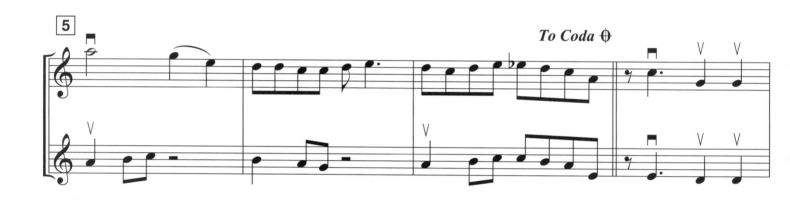

* The audio track for *Jazz Chaconne* is an extended loop of bars 9–16. Practice improvising using the rhythm and melodic riffs on page 47.

Jazz Chaconne Rhythm and Melodic Riffs

JAZZ RHYTHM RIFFS—*Echo back the swing rhythm riffs aurally or by reading on a pitch of your teacher's choice. Use the swing rhythm riffs to create a four- or eight-bar solo in bars 9–16 of the* Jazz Chaconne. *Create and write your own swing rhythm riff in the blank measures.*

JAZZ MELODIC RIFFS—*Echo back the melodic riffs by reading or aurally as played by your teacher. Use the melodic riffs to create a four- or eight-bar solo in bars 9–16 of the* Jazz Chaconne. *Create and write your own melodic riff in the blank measures.*

MELODIC RIFF BOWING/ARTICULATION VARIATIONS—*Echo back the melodic riff variations either by reading or aurally as played by your teacher. Each group of two bars has the same notes, but variations are created by adding new slurs, bowings, and articulations. Play line B to practice the rhythms that are created from the bowings in line A. Create and write your own bowing/articulation riff in the blank measures.*

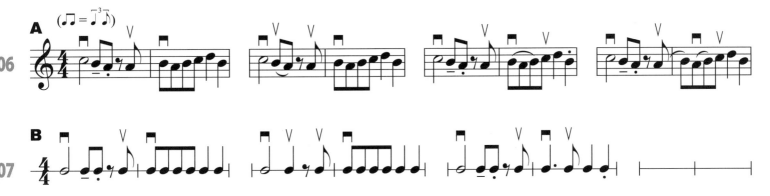

CREATIVITY ASSIGNMENT—*Play the rhythm and melodic riffs adding slurs, articulations, and different bowings as creative tools.*

Latin Chaconne

208 **LATIN CHACONNE**—*Expressively perform* Latin Chaconne *as directed by your teacher. At bar 9, create an improvised solo by using pitches from the A natural minor or A harmonic minor scale or by combining two-bar riffs from the rhythm and melodic riffs page. Compare and contrast the* Jazz *and* Latin Chaconne *discussing how their styles and genres differ. Discuss the periods and cultures they represent.*

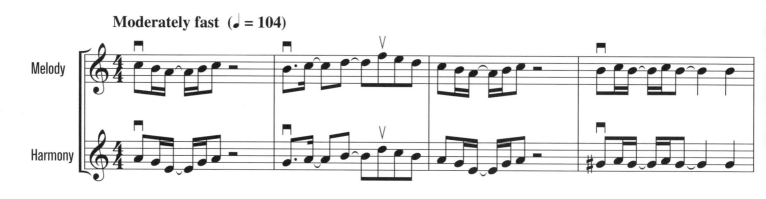

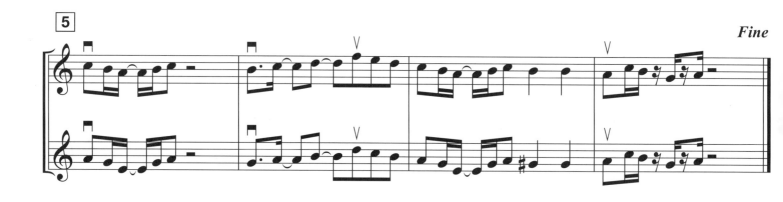

* The audio track for *Latin Chaconne* is an extended loop of bars 9–16. Practice improvising using the rhythm and melodic riffs on page 49.

Latin Chaconne Rhythm and Melodic Riffs

LATIN RHYTHM RIFFS—*Echo back the rhythm riffs aurally or by reading on a pitch of your teacher's choice. Use the rhythm riffs to create a four- or eight-bar solo in bars 9–16 of the Latin Chaconne. Create and write your own rhythm riff in the blank measures.*

LATIN MELODIC RIFFS—*Echo back the melodic riffs by reading or aurally as played by your teacher. Use the melodic riffs to create a four- or eight-bar solo in bars 9–16 of Latin Chaconne. Create and write your own melodic riff in the blank measures.*

MELODIC RIFF BOWING/ARTICULATION VARIATIONS—*Echo back the melodic riff variations either by reading or aurally as played by your teacher. Each group of two bars has the same notes, but variations are created by adding new slurs, bowings, and articulations. Play line B to practice the rhythms that are created from the bowings in line A. Create and write your own bowing/articulation riff in the blank measures.*

CREATIVITY ASSIGNMENT—*Play the rhythm and melodic riffs adding slurs, articulations, and different bowings as creative tools.*

Rock Chaconne

217 **ROCK CHACONNE**—*Expressively perform* Rock Chaconne *as directed by your teacher. At bar 9, create an improvised solo by using pitches from the A natural minor or A harmonic minor scale or by combining two-bar riffs from the rhythm and melodic riffs page. Compare and contrast the* Latin *and* Rock Chaconne *discussing how their styles and genres differ. Discuss the periods and cultures they represent.*

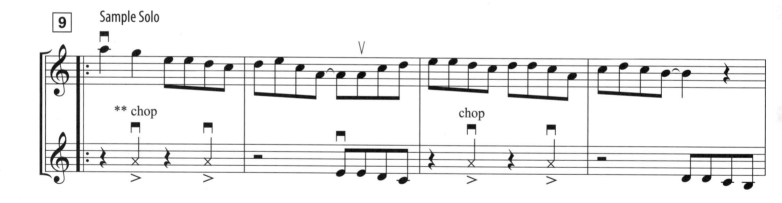

* The audio track for *Rock Chaconne* is an extended loop of bars 9–16. Practice improvising using the rhythm and melodic riffs on page 51.

** Play the chop notes by straightening your bow-hand thumb and rolling the stick of the bow toward your face. Use a wrist motion to slap the bow down with a slight motion toward the fingerboard (Violin/Viola) or bridge (Cello/Bass). A percussive sound will occur when the the hair contacts and sticks into the string.

Rock Chaconne Rhythm and Melodic Riffs

ROCK RHYTHM RIFFS—*Echo back the rhythm riffs aurally or by reading on a pitch of your teacher's choice. Use the rhythm riffs to create a four- or eight-bar solo in bars 9–16 of the Rock Chaconne. Create and write your own rhythm riff in the blank measures.*

ROCK MELODIC RIFFS—*Echo back the melodic riffs by reading or aurally as played by your teacher. Use the melodic riffs to create a four- or eight-bar solo in bars 9–16 of Rock Chaconne. Create and write down your own melodic riff in the blank measures.*

MELODIC RIFF BOWING/ARTICULATION VARIATIONS—*Echo back the melodic riff variations either by reading or aurally as played by your teacher. Each group of two bars has the same notes, but variations are created by adding new slurs, bowings, and articulations. Play line B to practice the rhythms that are created from the bowings in line A. Create and write your own bowing/articulation riff in the blank measures.*

CREATIVITY ASSIGNMENT—*Play the rhythm and melodic riffs adding slurs, articulations, and different bowings as creative tools.*

Chaconne Composition

Composers use a variety of musical ideas, or motives, to create a composition. They may use scales, bass lines, chords/harmonies, melodies, and rhythms to draft musical works.

226   **E HARMONIC MINOR SCALE**—*Play the E harmonic minor scale.*

227   **CHACONNE BASS LINE**—*Play the Chaconne bass line in E minor.*

Play 4x with Chaconne melody in E minor.

228   **CHACONNE CHORDS**—*Select one note from each three-note chord to create your own harmony part.*

Play 4x with Chaconne melody in E minor.

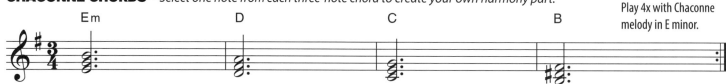

229   **CHACONNE RHYTHM RIFFS**—*Play the Chaconne rhythm riffs.*

230   **CHACONNE MELODY IN E MINOR**—*Create your own melody. Develop rhythmic passages for your melody by choosing rhythms from the Chaconne rhythm riffs. Choose pitches for your melody from the chord symbols above each bar, along with other scale tones. Preserve draft musical works through standard notation, audio, or video recording.*

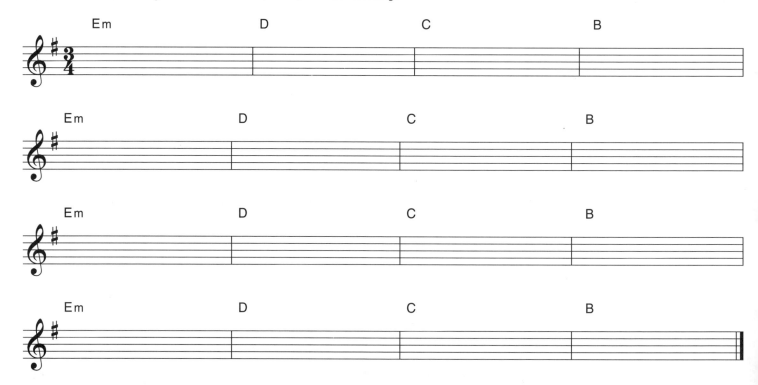

Play the melody you have written while your friends play the bass line or improvise a harmony part.

Taqsim No. 1 – Measured

TAQSIM—an instrumental form of Arabic and Turkish classical music guided by the makam/maqam system, a set of rules comparable to modes in Western music. Ordinarily improvised, taqsim consists of several sections and is usually nonmetric. The instrument plays either completely alone, with a percussionist, or with a drone.

31

TAQSIM NO. 1 MEASURED—*Expressively perform the* Taqsim No. 1 Measured *parts and repeats as assigned and directed by your teacher.*

* The audio track for *Taqsims No. 1–4* is a drone note. Listen and play along with the drone note to practice playing and improvising using the ideas in each taqsim.

Taqsim No. 2 – Unmeasured

232   **TAQSIM NO. 2 UNMEASURED**—*Play the* Taqsim No. 2 Unmeasured *parts and repeats as assigned and directed by your teacher.*

Taqsim No. 3 - Ordered Improvisation

233 **TAQSIM NO. 3 ORDERED IMPROVISATION**—*Perform the* Taqsim No. 3 Ordered Improvisation *parts as assigned and directed by your teacher. Use any or all of the pitches in each set to improvise for 5 to 10 seconds and then move on to the next set. Generate musical ideas by improvising, which is to create or perform spontaneously.*

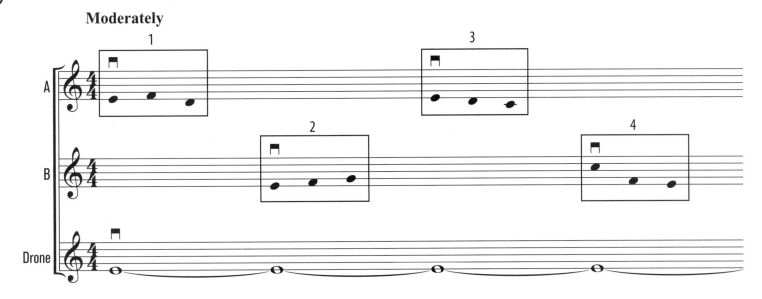

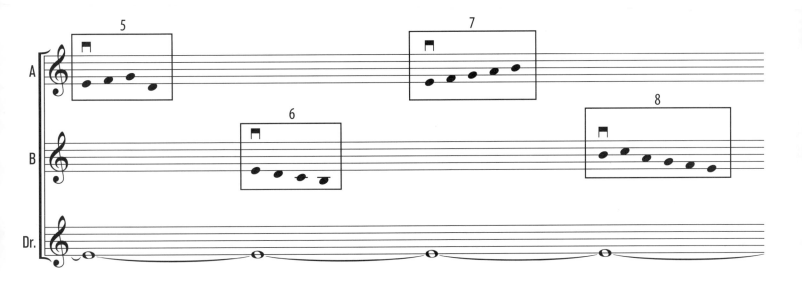

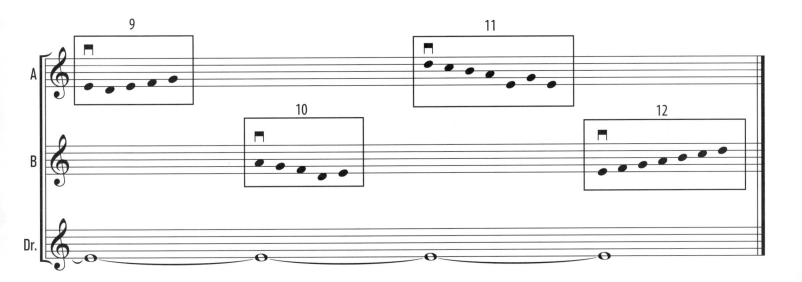

Taqsim No. 4 – Directed Improvisation

234 **TAQSIM NO. 4 DIRECTED IMPROVISATION**—*Compose your own Taqsim using the pitches E, F, G, A, B, C, D, E; then write it in music notation. Generate musical ideas by improvising, which is to create or perform spontaneously.*

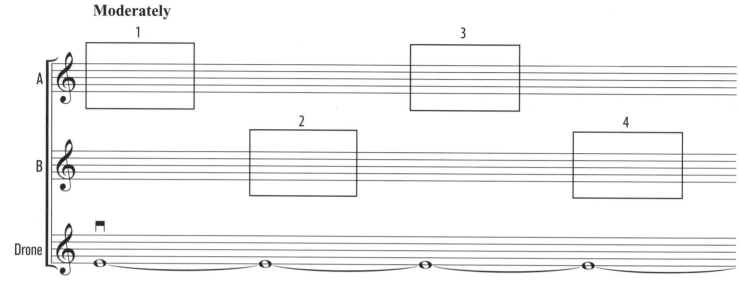
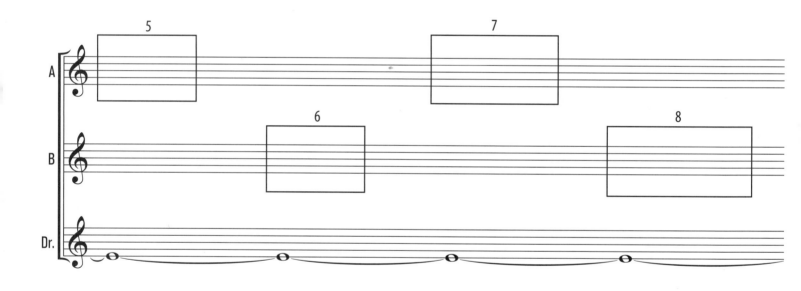
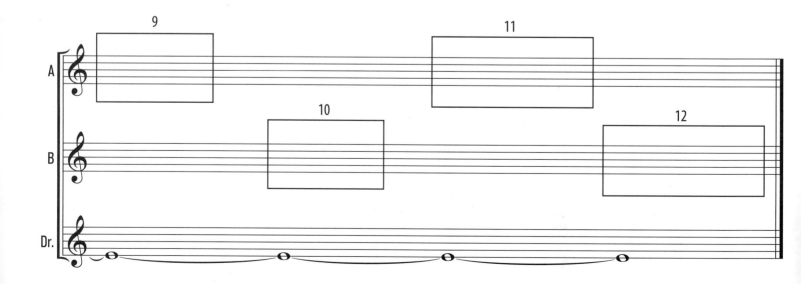